THE SIX LARGEST DESERTS IN THE WORLD!

GEOGRAPHY BOOKS FOR KIDS 5-7

Children's Geography Books

Speedy Publishing LLC
40 E. Main St. #1156
Newark, DE 19711
www.speedypublishing.com

In this book, we're going to talk about the six largest deserts in the world. So, let's get right to it!

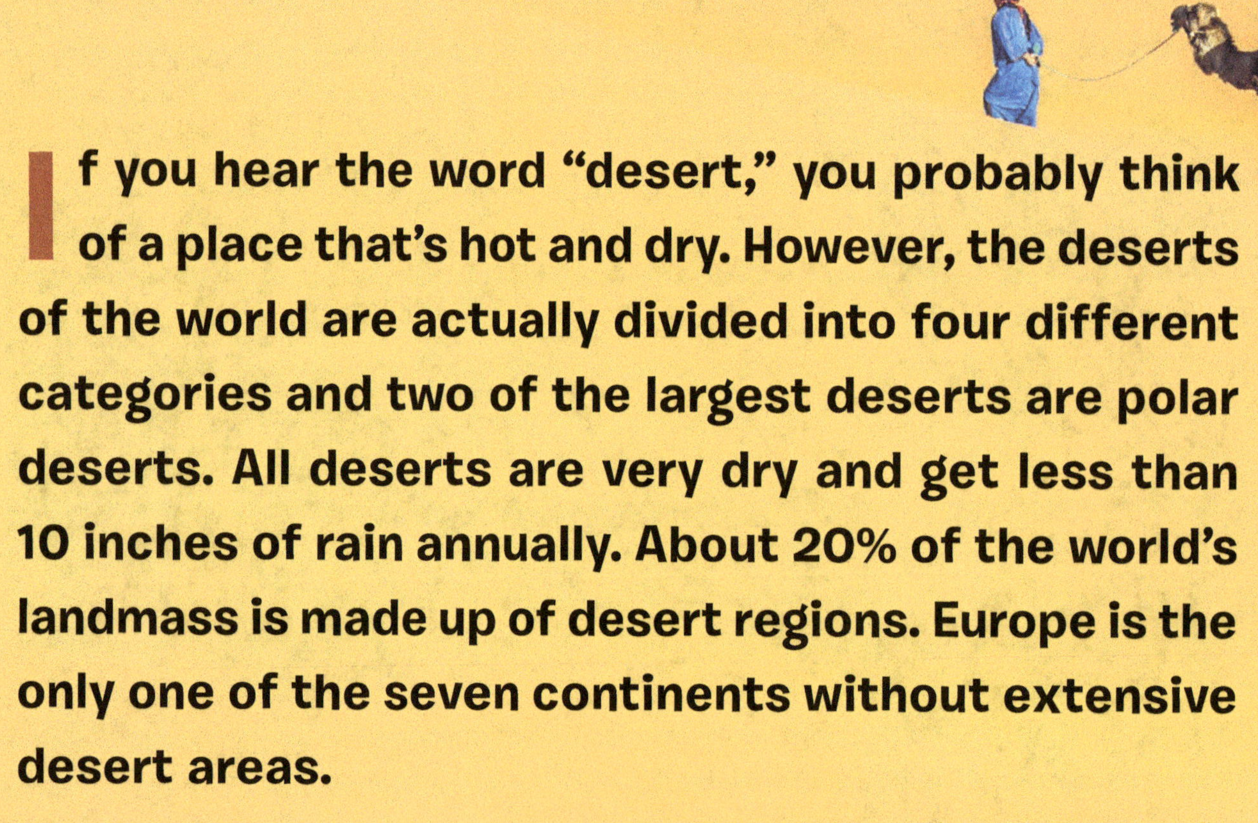

If you hear the word "desert," you probably think of a place that's hot and dry. However, the deserts of the world are actually divided into four different categories and two of the largest deserts are polar deserts. All deserts are very dry and get less than 10 inches of rain annually. About 20% of the world's landmass is made up of desert regions. Europe is the only one of the seven continents without extensive desert areas.

Here are the four different categories of deserts:

Subtropical – These are the hottest of the four desert regions. They have very dry terrain and any water that falls there evaporates very quickly.

Cool, coastal deserts – Even though these deserts are sometimes located in the same latitudes as the deserts that are subtropical, they are much cooler due to very cold ocean currents offshore, which cool down the land.

Cold winter deserts – These deserts are characterized by a huge range of temperatures depending on the season. In the summer, the temperatures can soar up to 100 degrees Fahrenheit. In the winter, they can drop to 10 degrees Fahrenheit.

Polar deserts – These polar regions are actually categorized as deserts since most of their moisture is frozen in ice.

SNOW DESERT WINTER LANDSCAPE IN ICELAND

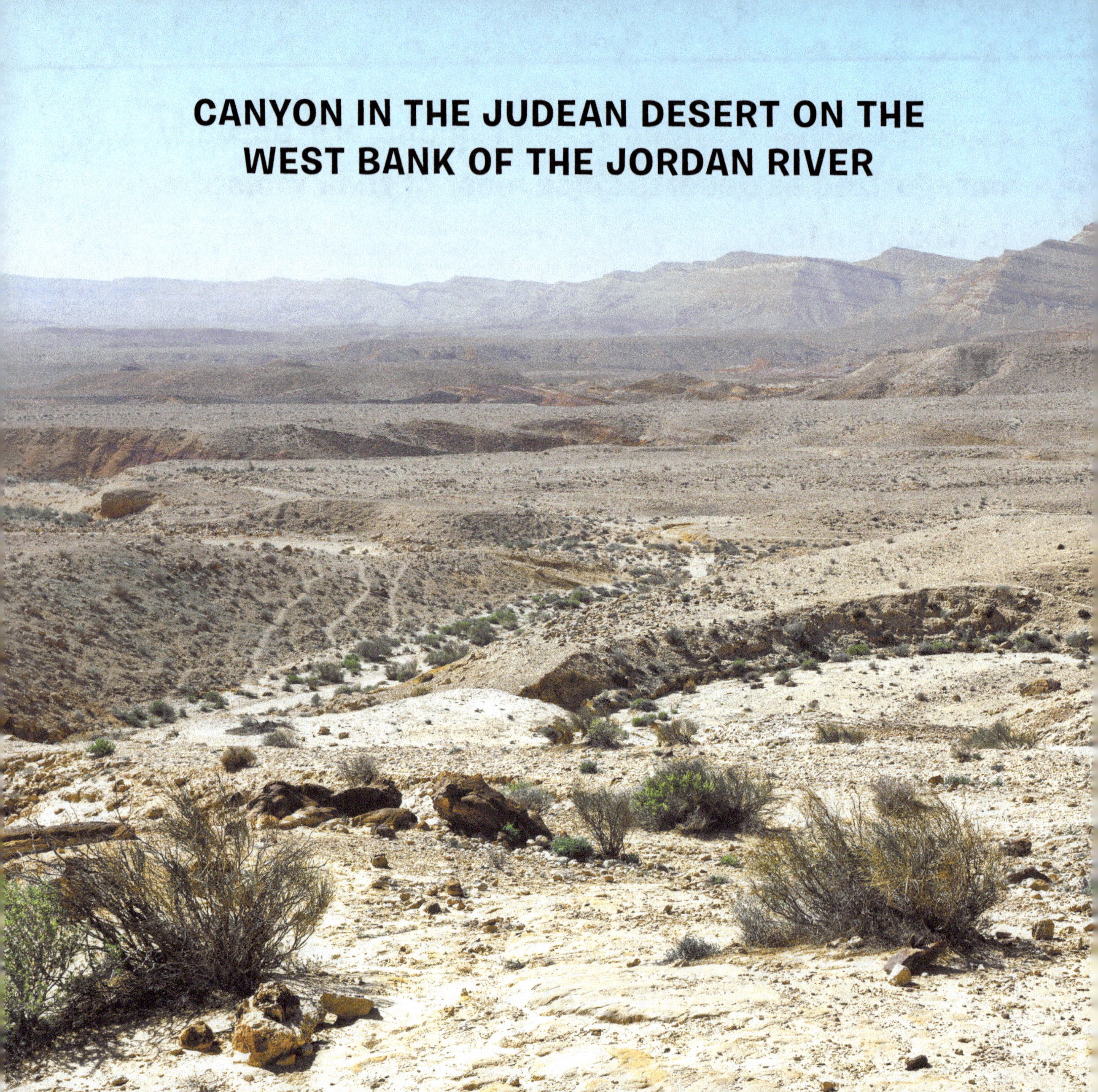

CANYON IN THE JUDEAN DESERT ON THE WEST BANK OF THE JORDAN RIVER

THE DESERT ENVIRONMENT

Some deserts are covered with sand, but most are not. Instead, they have rocky surfaces that have very few sand-size particles. The wind sweeps any such small pieces away, leaving a barren landscape. In polar deserts, the rocky surfaces are covered with thick layers of ice.

Because deserts get so little water, any surface streams usually only occur directly after rainfall unless the source of the water comes from an area outside the desert. Some of the stream's water evaporates quickly. Some is absorbed by the roots of plants and then released into the atmosphere, a process called transpiration. Any remaining water infiltrates into the ground. Some regions of polar desert haven't received any rain for over 2 million years.

LIZARD IN DESERT OF CENTRAL ASIA, KAZAKHSTAN

DESERT ANIMALS AND PLANTS

Animals and plants that live in the desert have adapted to an incredibly harsh environment. The plants in subtropical deserts must be able to tolerate the intense rays of the sun and go for very long periods of time with little to no water.

Plants that survive have unique ways to prevent the loss of moisture even within huge temperature ranges from very cold to very hot. They must also be able to survive dry, high-speed winds and an atmosphere with almost no humidity.

Desert animals that live in non-polar deserts must be able to deal with temperature extremes and be able to survive with almost no water. Animals that live in the hotter deserts cope by staying underground and then hunting by night.

ICE PLAIN IN ICELAND

THE SIX LARGEST DESERTS

There are deserts on all seven continents of the world. The six largest deserts are:

- The Antarctic desert, which is located in Antarctica and is a polar desert
- The Arctic desert, which is located at the Arctic Circle and is a polar desert

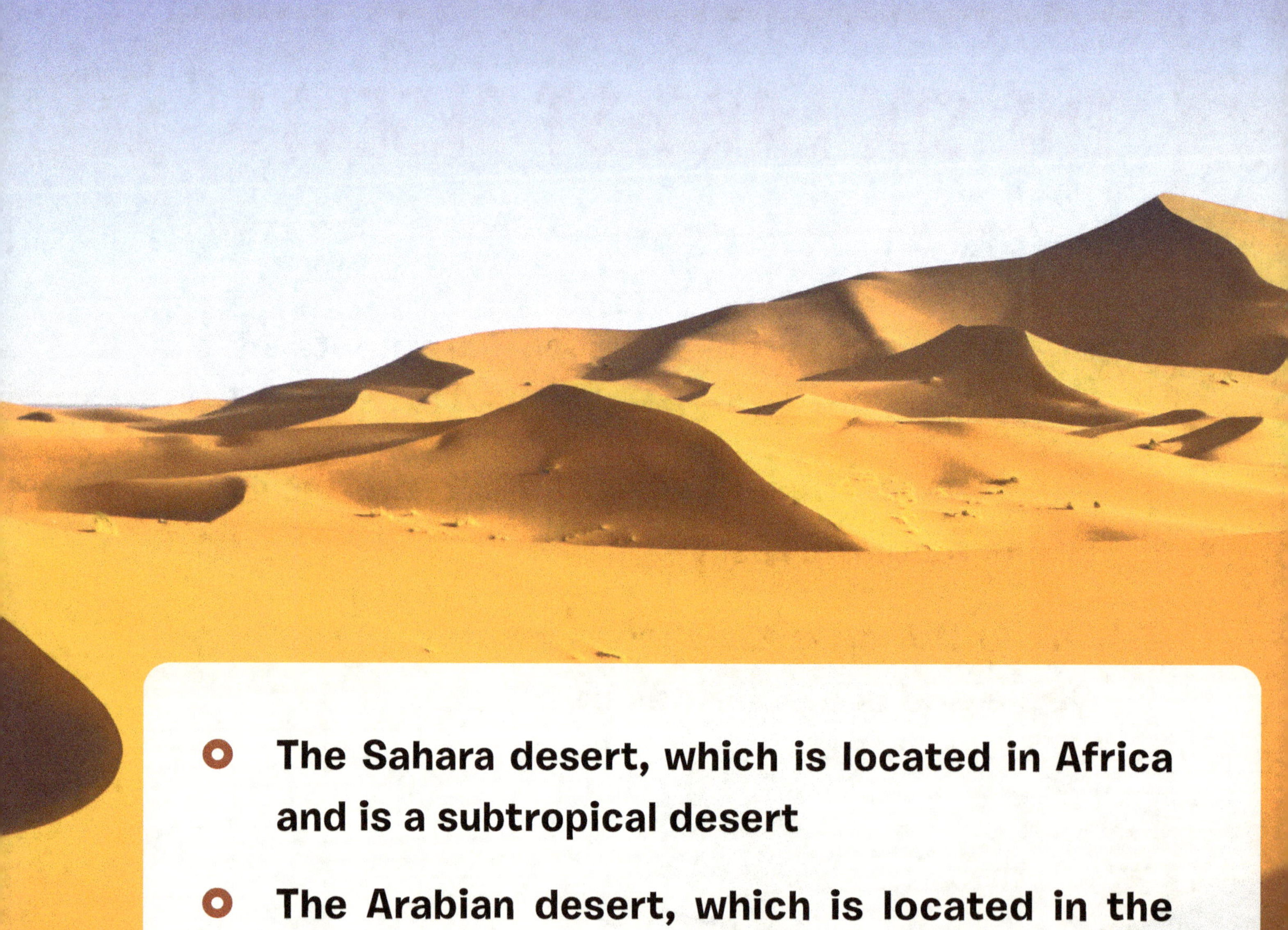

- The Sahara desert, which is located in Africa and is a subtropical desert
- The Arabian desert, which is located in the Middle East and is a subtropical desert

SAHARA DESERT

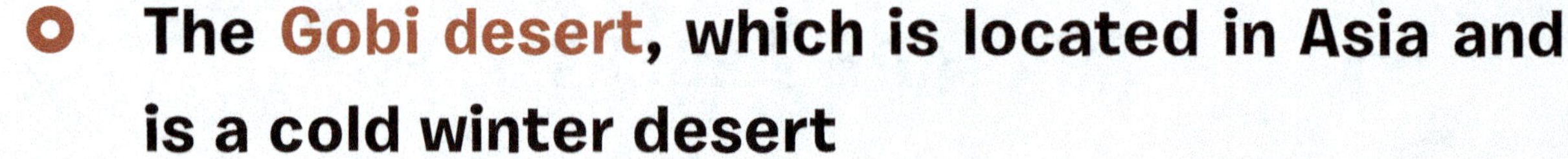

- The Gobi desert, which is located in Asia and is a cold winter desert

- The Kalahari desert, which is located in Africa and is a subtropical desert

ANTARCTIC DESERT

THE ANTARCTIC DESERT

The Antarctic Desert covers an area that is a staggering 5.5 million square miles. It's so big that it has an area that's larger than the combined totals of the other deserts in this group, except for the Arctic. It gets less than 2 inches of precipitation every year and some of its valleys haven't had any rain for a very long time—at least a period of 2 million years!

The terrain is bedrock mixed with massive boulders and plains of gravel. The Dry Valleys have frozen lakes that are filled with salt. The Don Juan Pond is located there. It is the saltiest water on Earth with a saline level of 40%.

The average temperature during the winter is minus 20 degrees Fahrenheit, but it can go down to minus 90. During the summer, there's almost 24 hours of full daylight and the temperature goes up to 30 degrees Fahrenheit.

It was thought for a long time that these areas had no life at all. However, in the 1970s, scientists found quite a few microorganisms living there. Since that time almost 350 species of vascular plants have been found, so about 5% of the polar desert is covered with some type of flora. The tallest shrubs don't get taller than three feet.

Animals living there, such as penguins, seals, and seabirds, depend on the surrounding waters for their food.

THE ARCTIC DESERT

The Arctic Desert covers an area that is almost as large as the Antarctic desert, 5.4 million square miles. Sections of the Arctic Desert are located above 75 degrees north latitude. The North Pole, Melvin Island, Severny Island, and sections of Greenland are all regions of the Arctic Desert.

ARCTIC DESERT

The Alaskan portion of the United States and portions of Canada are part of the Arctic Desert. The countries of Norway and Sweden as well as Finland and Russia all have sections in this polar desert, which is composed of tundra, snow, and glaciers. One of the most interesting things about the Arctic Desert is that during the summer the sun doesn't go down. It's poised over the horizon.

THE SAHARA DESERT

The Sahara Desert covers an area that is 3.5 million square miles. This desert is the largest of the non-polar deserts. Located in North Africa, it stretches from the Atlantic Ocean in the west direction to the Red Sea at the east. South of the desert is an area called the Sahel Region.

SAHARA DESERT

It is situated between the desert and the savanna. The Sahara Desert is so large that it covers regions of eleven different African countries. If the Sahara were a country, it would be ranked fifth in the world, because it has a size that's almost equivalent to the continental United States.

The Sahara is one of the hottest places on the face of the Earth. Sometimes temperatures there are hotter than 120 degrees Fahrenheit for a week or more. The hottest temperature ever recorded there was 136 degrees Fahrenheit! Despite these very hot temperatures, at night, the temperature can go below freezing. Some regions go for years on end with not one drop of rain.

The Sahara has several different types of landforms including dunes, which are hills of sand, and hamadas, which are rocky plateaus with no vegetation. Some sand dunes can reach more than 500 feet in height. Because of the harsh conditions, only about 2.5 million people live in the Sahara.

THE ARABIAN DESERT

The Arabian Desert covers an area that is 1 million square miles. It is the second largest desert that falls in the non-polar category. The center section of this desert is one of the largest regions of the world with continuous sands. It is called the Rub'al-Khali and is nicknamed the "Empty Quarter" because sand is the only surface feature there. There are vast sources of oil in this region.

ARABIAN DESERT

THE GOBI DESERT

Surrounded by Mongolian grasslands and the range of the Altai Mountains, the Gobi Desert covers an area that is 500,000 square miles and is the largest desert region in Asia. It is situated in the north part of China, as well as Mongolia, and is located on a high plateau. Because it is so far above sea level at 3,000 feet, it is a cold desert.

SAXAUL IN GOBI DESERT

It's known for the important cities that were benchmarks along the historical trade route called the Silk Road during the time of the great Mongolian Empire.

287

RIDING A CAMEL IN GOBI DESERT

The Gobi Desert has one of the most extreme climates in the world. The temperature changes rapidly, both daily and by season. In the summer months, the temperatures go up to 122 degrees Fahrenheit.

In the winter, they can drop lower than minus 40 degrees Fahrenheit. The Gobi is still growing and this is sounding an alarm bell for the Chinese since they are losing valuable grasslands as a result. They are currently planting a line of forest called the "Green Wall of China" to prevent the desert from expanding further.

CRESCENT BAY IN CHINA

KALAHARI DESERT

THE KALAHARI DESERT

The Kalahari Desert covers an area that is 360,000 square miles. Located in the southern portion of Africa, the Kalahari Desert has huge temperature fluctuations.

Temperatures can drop to zero at nighttime, but soar to 104 degrees Fahrenheit during the day. The Kalahari actually has huge grazing areas that are suitable for supporting some types of animals, such as the Oryx gazelle.

Awesome! Now you know more about the six largest deserts in the world. You can find more Geography books from Baby Professor by searching the website of your favorite book retailer.

www.ingramcontent.com/pod-product-compliance
Lightning Source LLC
LaVergne TN
LVHW060828170826
845678LV00010B/1931

* 9 7 9 8 8 6 9 4 3 1 6 3 9 *